Hidden Pictures

GRADES 2-4

This book has been correlated to state, national, and Canadian provincial standards. Visit *www.carsondellosa.com* to search for and view its correlations to your standards.

Credits

Editors: Carrie Fox and Kelly Warfield
Layout and Cover Design: Lori Jackson
Inside Illustrations: Lori Jackson
Cover Photo: © Arvind Balaraman

ISBN 978-1-60418-142-5
03-147131151

Table of Contents

About This Book

Graphing Hidden Pictures is a book of challenging, self-correcting graph paper activities designed for students in second, third, and fourth grade. In each activity, students are guided to color graph paper squares one by one, causing a "hidden picture" to gradually appear. At first, you may need to work closely with students on these activities. Student independence will increase with experience.

Student Goals

- To develop and strengthen graphing skills
- To develop fine-motor skill coordination
- To employ transference
- To reinforce the ability to follow directions
- To enhance concentration skills and attention to details

Teacher Directions

1. Make a copy of the blank graph reproducible (page 64) and a directions page for each student. (Be sure to make extra copies of the blank graph reproducible because students may make errors when first learning this activity.)

2. Have students color each square on the graph paper by following the information supplied on the directions page for each picture. For example, when a direction reads "Color [R] K8," each student should locate column K at the bottom of the page with one finger on her right hand and row 8 on the left of the page with a finger on her left hand. The student should move her fingers along the column and row until they meet at square K8. Then, she should color the square red (based on the color key at the top of the page). When a direction indicates to color a specific square [B/Gn], the student should color half of the square blue and half of the square green.

Hints for Success

- Tell each student to cross out each direction on the directions page as he has colored the corresponding squares on his blank graph paper. Another helpful hint is to have the student fold back or cover each row of directions as he completes it.

- After each student has colored an entire graph, you may want to show her the answer key to help her add faces and other details.

- Encourage students to make their pictures more attractive by:

    a. applying colors solidly with crayons or markers and staying within the lines.

    b. blending together squares of the same color rather than outlining individual squares.

Y = yellow   Gn = green   R = red

Color [Gn]	B3	F3	H6	C3	E6	G3	K3	
Color [R/Y/Gn]	B7	D7	F7	H7	J7			
Color [Y/Gn]	K4	E4	A4	G4	I4	C4		
Color [Y/Gn/R]	A7	C7	E7	G7	I7	K7		
Color [Gn]	H3	A6	D3	I6	E3	C6	J6	B6
Color [Gn/Y/R]	A2	C2	E2	G2	I2	K2		
Color [Gn/Y]	A5	C5	E5	G5	I5	K5		
Color [Gn/Y]	B5	D5	F5	H5	J5			
Color [Gn/Y/R]	B2	D2	F2	H2	J2			
Color [Y/R]	B1	D1	F1	H1	J1			
Color [Y/R]	A8	C8	E8	G8	I8	K8		
Color [Y/R]	B8	D8	F8	H8	J8			
Color [R/Y]	A1	C1	E1	G1	I1	K1		
Color [Y/Gn]	B4	D4	F4	H4	J4			
Color [Gn]	K6	A3	F6	G6	I3	J3	D6	

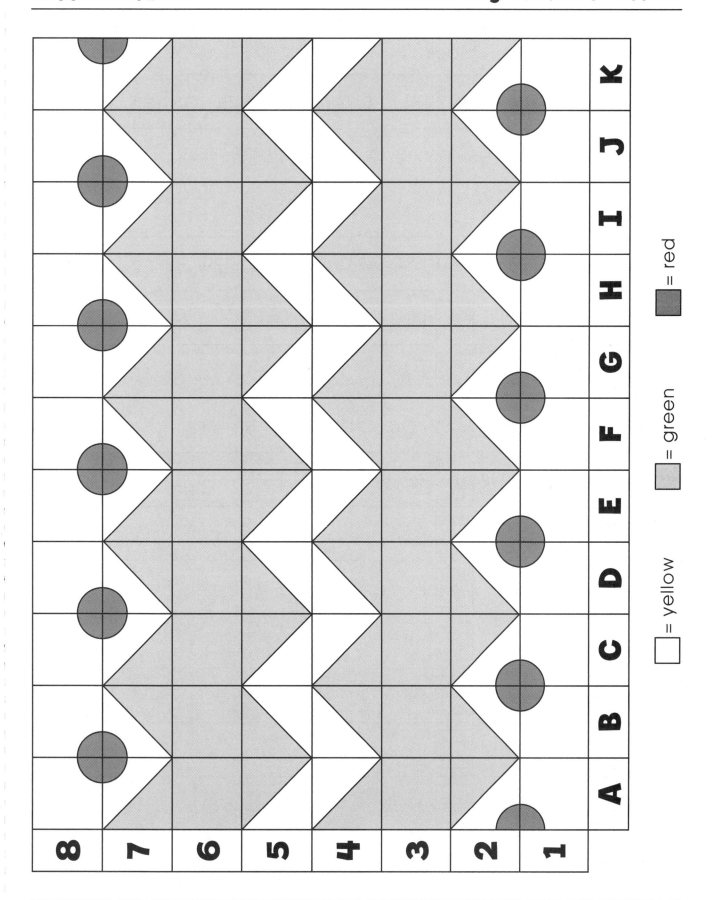

= red

= green

= yellow

W = white   Y = yellow   Gy = gray   Gn = green
B = blue   Bk = black

Color [B]	C1	H4	K6	I7	K1	H5	J6	K8	G1	F1	G3	G5	K5	H1
Color [W]	F8	C6	D5	D3	I2	G2	[Gn/Y]	B5	B6					
Color [Gy]	E6	E5	F5	[Y/B/W] I4									
Color [Gn]	A2	B8	B3	A8	B1	A7	A3	B7	A1	B4	B2			
Color [W/B] C3		[B/W] K4		[Gy/B] F6									
Color [Bk/W] J3		[B/W] C7		[Y/Gn/Y] A5									
Color [W]	C5	E3	D7	E2	D6	C4	D4	F2	H2	I3			
Color [B]	I6	K7	J8	J1	H6	I8	[B/W] E8						
Color [Gn/Y] A6		[W/B] F3		[B/W] H3									
Color [Gy/B] F7	F4	[W/B] K2		[Gy/W] E4									
Color [Y/B] I5		[Y/Gn] A4		[W/B] J2									
Color [W/B] G8		[B/W] D8		[W/B] K3									
Color [B/W] C2		[W/Gy] E7											
Color [W/B] D2		[B/W] J4											
Color [B]	G4	J5	H7	G6	J7	I1	G7	C8	H8	D1	E1			

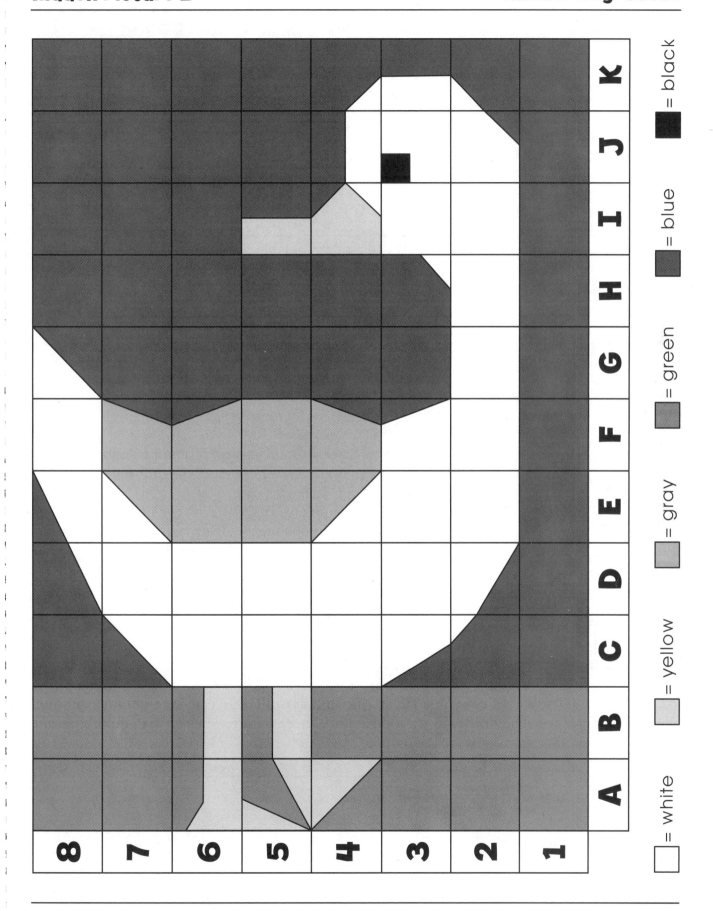

W = white   LB = light blue   Y = yellow   R = red
DB = dark blue   Br = brown

Color [LB] A4 G8 B6 H7 K3 J5 B4 C5 A5 H8 B7 C6 A3 K4

Color [R] E4 D4 E5 E6   [Y/DB] D2 F2 H2

Color [DB] G1 H4 G6 D1 G4 C1 F6 H1 K1 E1 F4 B1 J1

Color [LB/DB] F8 H6 J4   [LB/R] D6 E8 C4

Color [Y/LB/DB] J2   [R/LB] C3

Color [LB/Y/DB] C2   [LB/DB] B2

Color [W] G5 F7 F5 H5   [LB/W] I5 G7

Color [LB] B5 J3 I8 C7 A6 H3 J6 A7 C8 D8 G3 I6 K5 K6

Color [Br|LB] F3

Color [LB/R] D5 E7

Color [R/LB] D3 E3

Color [LB/DB] A2 K2

Color [Y/DB] I2 G2 E2

Color [DB] A1 I4 F1 I1

Color [LB] D7 A8 J8 I7 K8 B3 B8 J7 K7 I3

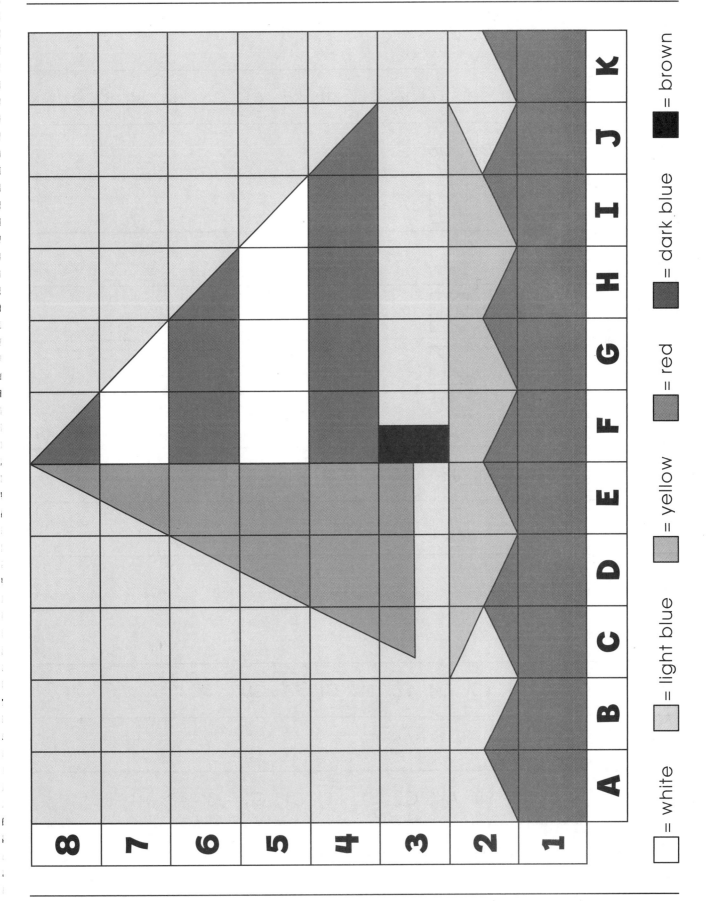

W = white   Pk = pink   R = red

Color	[R]	A6 B4 H8 I7 J6 E8 K4 K5 A1 C8 H3 I4 B7 D1
Color	[Pk]	I2 B2 D5 D6 G7 C6
Color	[R|W]	B6 B5 [Pk|R] J7
Color	[Pk/R/W]	E2 C4 D3
Color	[R/Pk]	A7 [Pk|R] J2
Color	[W|R]	I5 I6 [R/W/Pk] C7 F7
Color	[Pk/W/R]	H4 G3 F2
Color	[R]	I8 B8 F1 J5 K3 A5 C3 K1 D2 B1 G2 I1 A3 H2
Color	[R/W]	G8 D8 [R/Pk] I3 B3
Color	[R|Pk]	A2
Color	[R]	K6 K7 K8
Color	[Pk]	E5 F3 D7 D4 E6 E4 F4 F6 G4
Color	[W/R/Pk]	E7 H7
Color	[R]	J4 E1 F8 A4 C2 J1 K2 C1 G1 J3 A8 H1 J8
Color	[Pk]	C5 E3 H6 H5 G5 G6 F5

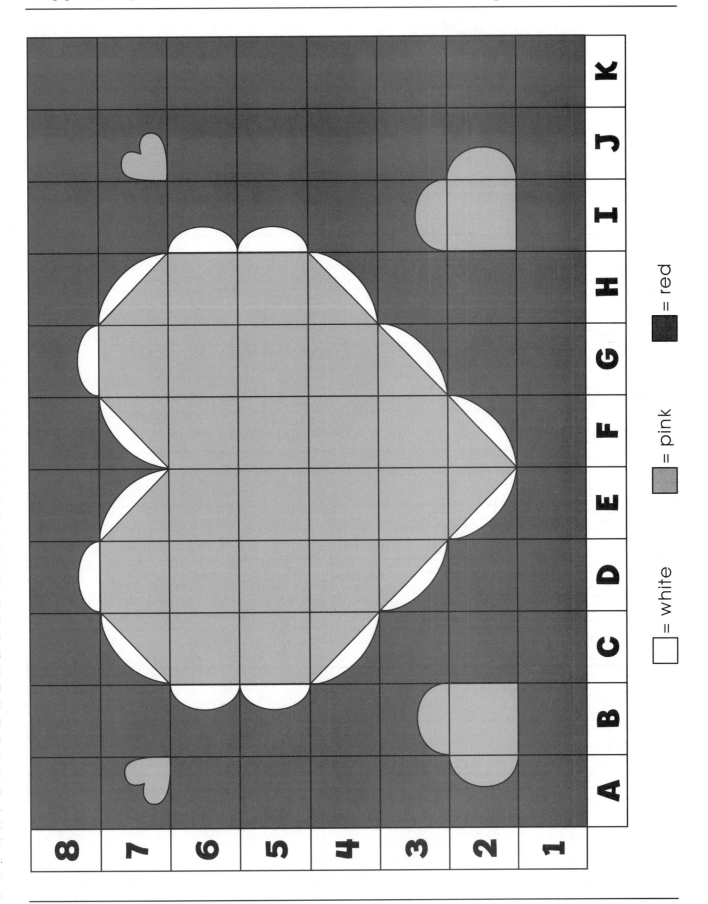

B = blue   LG = light green   DG= dark green   R = red
S = silver

Color	R	H6 E7 F5 D6 E4 D8 G4 H7 D7 F6 F7 G7 H8
Color	B	A8 C7 A1 I8 K5 B7 F1 J8 F2 I1 A2 K6 J2 B6
Color	LG	D2 B4 C5 C4 D3 D4 C3 D5
Color	DG	H2 J4 I4 H3 I3 I5 H4 H5
Color	[LG/DG/B] F3 [B/R] G8 [R/DG] G3
Color	[B/R] E8 [R/DG] G5
Color	[LG/B] D1 A4 C2
Color	B	B2 C8 I7 A3 K7 C1 B1 J6 K8 A7 K1 E1 A5 F8
Color	[R/R/DG] G6 [DG/S/B] J3
Color	[S/B] B3 [LG/R] E5
Color	[R/LG] E3 [B/DG] I6 J5
Color	[B/LG] C6 B5 [DG/B] G2
Color	[LG/B] E2 [DG/B] H1 I2 K4
Color	[R/LG] F4 [R/LG/R] E6
Color	B	J7 K2 B8 G1 A6 J1 K3

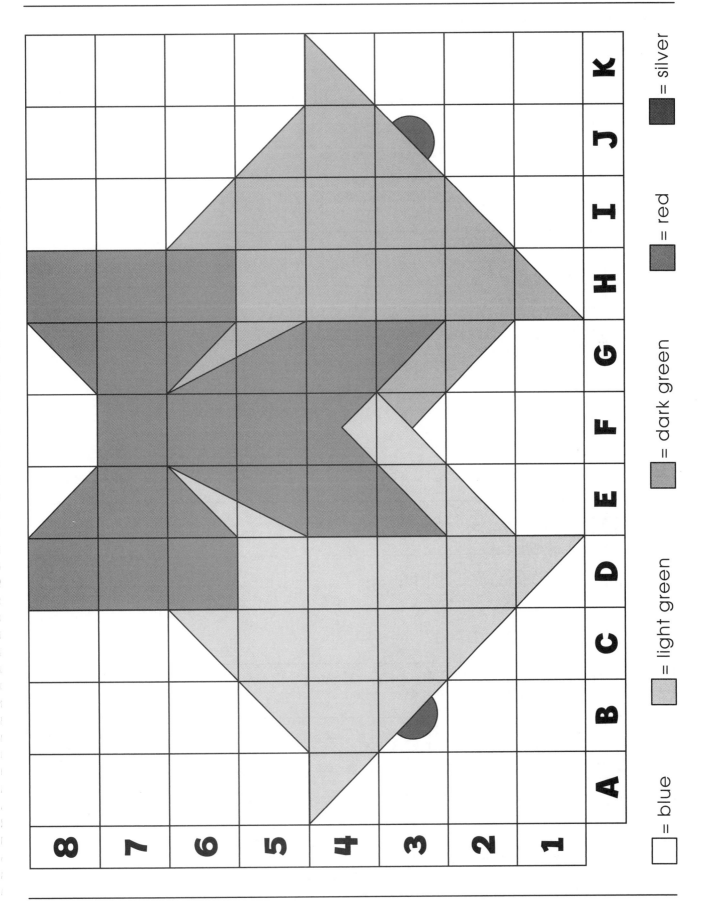

O = orange   Y = yellow   R = red   Gn = green
Br = brown   Bk = black

Color [O] B8 J8 G8 BI AI A5 I8 A6 H8 K7 K4 KI J2 B2

Color [Br] FI CI EI H2 HI GI G2 C3 D3 H3 I3 G3 F3

Color [Bk] F5 F6 F4    I6 H6

Color [Br/O] C2   C6 D6   [R|O] E6

Color [Br/O] J3   [R|O|R] C4 C5 D4 D5

Color [Br/O] I2   F8   [O/Bk/O] F7

Color [Br/O] B3   [Y/O] J7 E7

Color [O] A4 C8 E8 JI K5 K6 A3 D8 A7 K8 K3 A8 A2 K2

Color [Gn/O/Gn] H4 H5 I4 I5

Color [O/Y] B7 G7   [O|R] B4 B5

Color [O/Y/Y] C7 D7 H7 I7

Color [Gn/O] J5 J4   [O|R] B6

Color [O/Gn] G4 G5   [O/Gn] G6

Color [Br] DI E2 II F2 D2 E3

Color [R|O] E4 E5   J6

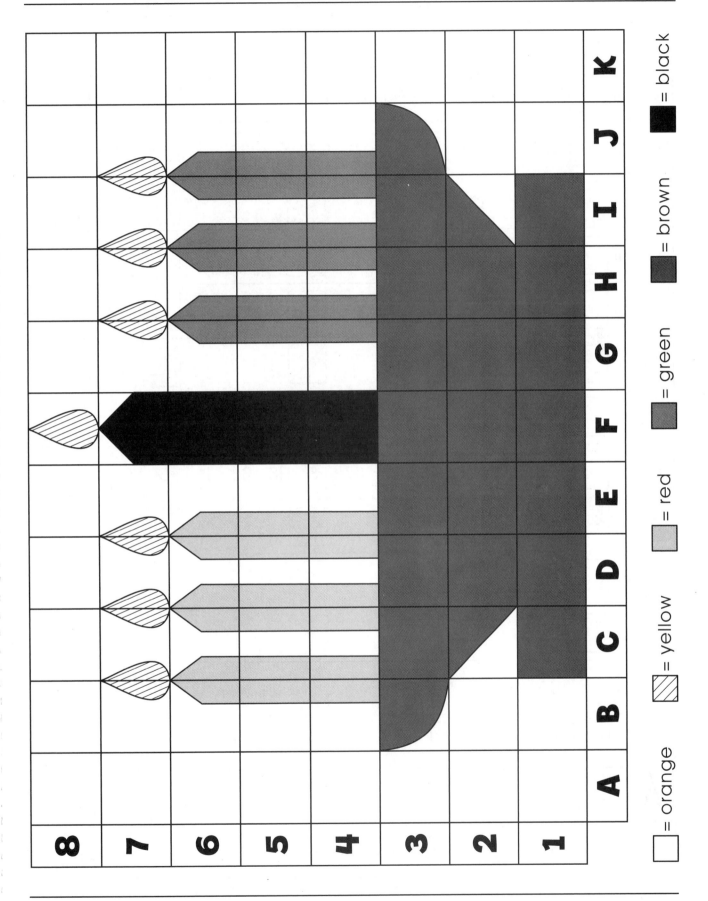

Y = yellow   B = blue   Gn = green   R = red
Br = brown   Bk = black

Color [Gn]   C5   K6   B1   K7   A8   B5   A6   C1   G7   B8   K8   D5   B6   H7

Color [B]   D4   F2   G5   F1   D2   F4   G6   G4   G2   [B|Y|B]   E1   H6

Color [Bk]   B4   B2   C2   C4   [Bk|B/Y] E3   [Br|Bk] I3

Color [R]   E7   F7   E6   D7   E8   [Gn/B] K5   [B/Gn] G1

Color [Br]   C7   B7   A7   A2   A4   H3   [B/Gn] K1   [Gn/Bk/Bk] C3

Color [Gn/Br/Bk] I5   [Gn/B] J1   [Gn/Br/Bk] H2   [Br/Bk/Gn] I1

Color [Gn/Bk] H1   [Bk|B] J2   J4   E4   E2

Color [Gn]   C8   I8   G8   A3   C6   J7   E5   H8   B3   J6   F5   I7   J8

Color [Gn/Bk] H5   [Br/Gn] I6   [Bk/B] J3   [Br/Gn] D1

Color [B/Y/B] G3   [Gn/R] D8   [R/Gn] F6

Color [Bk/Bk/Br] I2   [Gn/Br] A5   [Gn/Bk/Br] H4

Color [B|Y] D3   F3   [Gn/B] J5   [Br/Bk/Bk] I4

Color [Br/Gn] A1   [Gn/R] F8

Color [R/Gn] D6   [B|Gn] K4   K3   K2

Turn the paper. Draw a nose and a mouth. Write STOP on the sign.

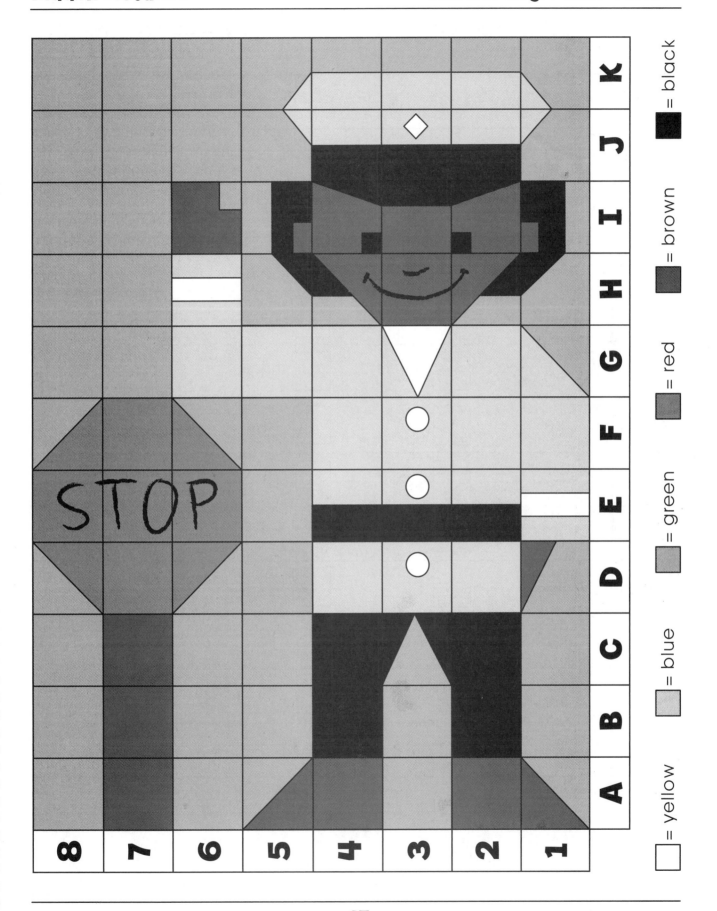

Hidden Picture 8 Directions

Y = yellow   LG = light green   T = tan   DG = dark green
Br = brown

Color G2 K4 E2 B7 A4 K2 E8 C8 A5 D2 B8

Color C1 G4 F1 I1 C4 A1 D1 H4 G1 J1

Color E7 E6 H3 B5 F5

Color C5 B1 K1 E1 B4 H1

Color C6 D6 G5 G6 B3 K7

Color I2 C2 J8 J4

Color K8 C7 H5

Color F6  G7 D5

Color A3 I8 B6 F7

Color J5 D7 H7

Color I3 D3 E3 F3

Color DG I6 B2 D4 F4 E5 I5 J7 H2 E4 I4 I7 J6

Color Y K3 G8 A7 J2 F8 A2 J3 A8 A6 H8 F2 K5 D8

Color G3 C3 K6 H6

Draw eyes and a mouth.

© Carson-Dellosa • CD-104283   **18**   Graphing Hidden Pictures

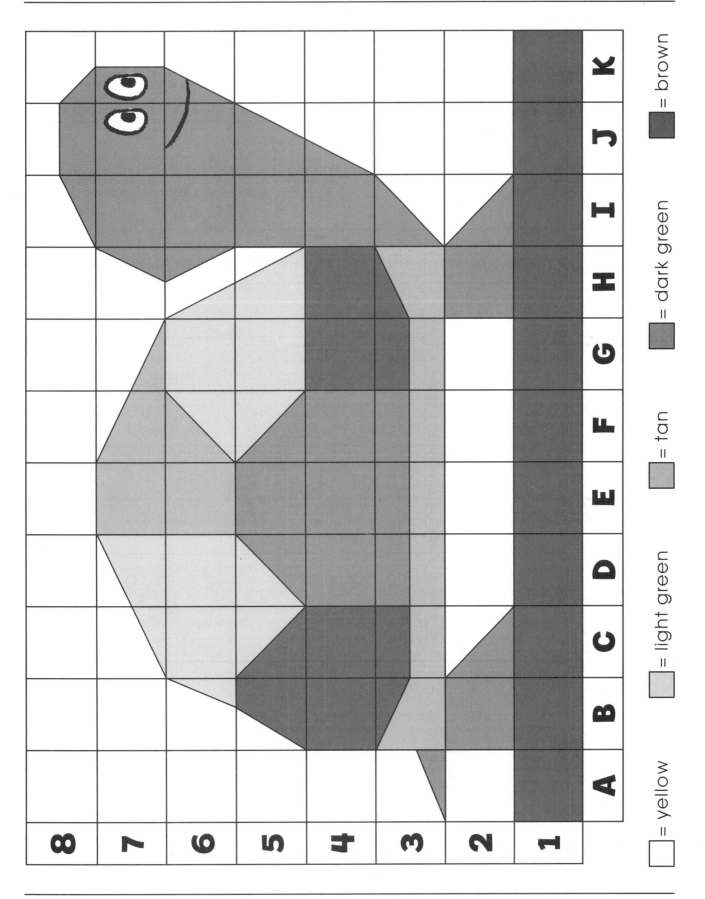

W = white   LB = light blue   Gy = gray   DB = dark blue
Bk = black

Color [DB] D1 B1 A1 C1 A2 F1

Color [W] K2 I1 K3 A4 K4 J1 I5 I4

Color [LB] J8 A7 B6 G7 B5 A6 E8 C5 I8 K8 D8 C6 H7

Color [W|Gy] D4 H3 H6 C4 B2

Color F6 E3 F2 H2 E5 G3 E6 F3 E4 E7

Color D2 G5 F7 F5 I2

Color G2 B4 E2 G4

Color F4 G1 D7 D5 C2

Color J4 D3

Color [LB] B7 G6 A8 I7 F8 H8 J6 C8 K7 C7 B8 G8 J7 K6

Color H1 D6

Color [W] H4 B3 J2 H5 K1 J5 A3 J3 C3

Color E1 K5 A5 I6

Color I3

Draw a mouth, a nose, eyes, and whiskers.

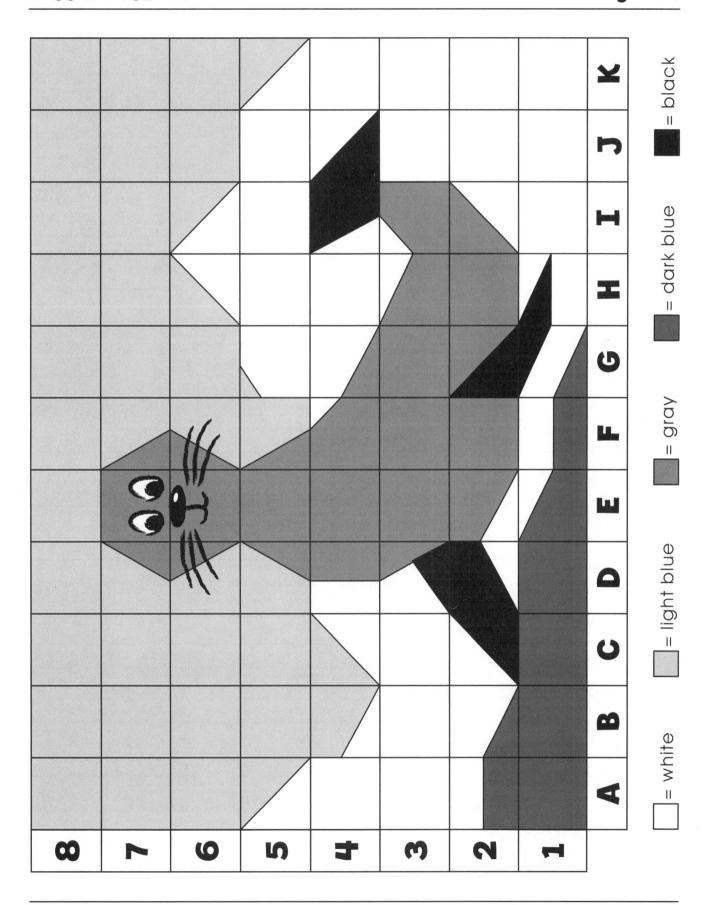

Hidden Picture 10

Directions

Pk = pink   O = orange   Gn = green   B = blue   Bk = black

Color	[B]	D8 J8 G8 D7 K7 B8 I8 A7 F8 B7 DI K8
Color	[Pk/Gn]	H4
Color	[B|Gn]	B2 HI A2 EI [O/B/Bk] G3
Color	[B/O]	H7 C4 [O] G6 G7 E2 E3
Color	[Gn/B]	H3 E5 A4 AI
Color	[B/Pk]	A6 I5 [Pk/B] D5 I4 [Pk/B/Bk] D6
Color	[B/Gn]	F5 B4 I3 K6 J3 [Gn|B] J2
Color	[Pk/B/Gn]	A5 [Gn/B/Gn] B3 [O/B] CI G2 H6
Color	[O/B]	C3 F6 I6 [B/Gn/B] K3 K5 JI
Color	[Pk]	F3 H5 C6 C5 F2 [Pk/B] D2 B5 J4 G4
Color	[B/Gn]	E6 A3 H2 E4
Color	[B/Pk]	B6 J5 D3 [B/O/Bk] F7 [B/Pk/Bk] G5
Color	[Gn/B]	F4 KI I2
Color	[B]	A8 C7 C8 E7 E8 FI GI II H8 J6 J7 D4
Color	[B/Gn/B]	BI K2 K4 [B/O] I7 C2

© Carson-Dellosa • CD-104283   **22**   Graphing Hidden Pictures

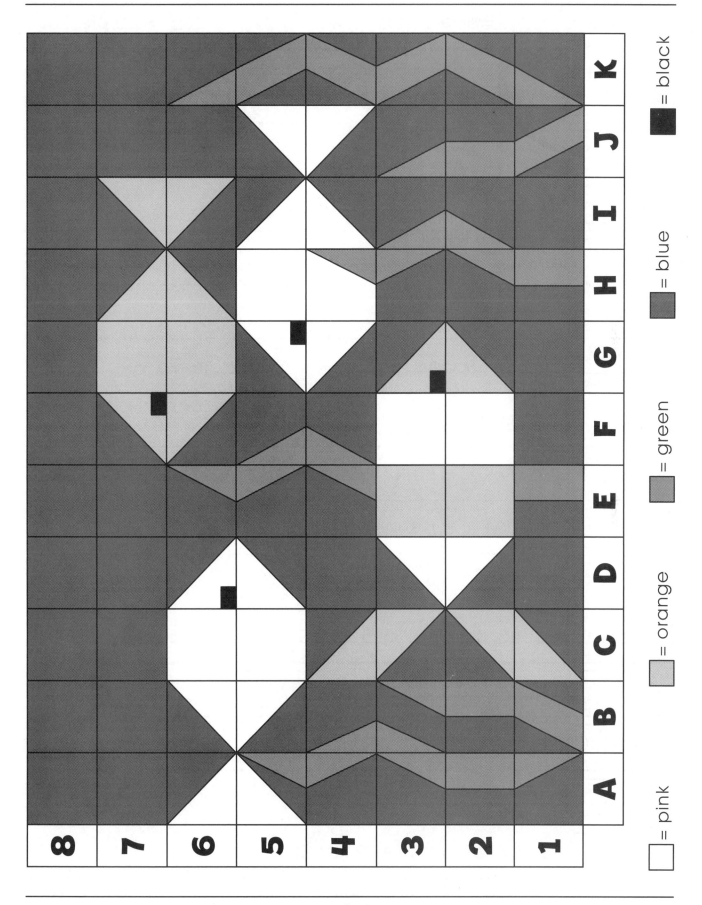

Y = yellow   S = silver   Gy = gray   Pl = purple
Bk = black

Color	[Pl]	E8 D5 K8 J5 C4 K2 E5 C8 K5 G8 H5 A4 B5

Color [Y] E3 F3 G3 H3 A7 H7

Color [Bk] E1 F1 C1 G1 D1 H1 I1 B1 A1 K1 J1

Color [Pl/Y] B3   [S/Gy/Pl] D2   [Y/Pl] K3

Color [Pl/Y] A3   [Pl/Y/Gy/S] C3   [Pl–S/Bk] F4

Color [Pl/Y/Gy] D6 G6 B6 A6 E6 J6 K6 C6 H6 I6 F6

Color [Y/Gy/S] D3 J3   [Y/Bk/Pl] B2

Color [Y/Pl] A2   [Pl/Y] H4

Color [Pl/Y] D4   [Pl/Y/Pl] K4

Color [Pl/Y] E4   [S/Gy/Pl] J2

Color [Pl] J8 A5 D8 I4 F8 I5 I8 G5 B4 A8 C5 H8 F5 B8

Color [Bk/Y/Pl] E2 F2 G2 H2

Color [Y/Gy/S] I3   [Pl/Y] J4

Color [Pl/Y] G4   [Y/Gy/S/Pl] C2 I2

Color [Y] E7 D7 B7 I7 F7 C7 J7 G7 K7

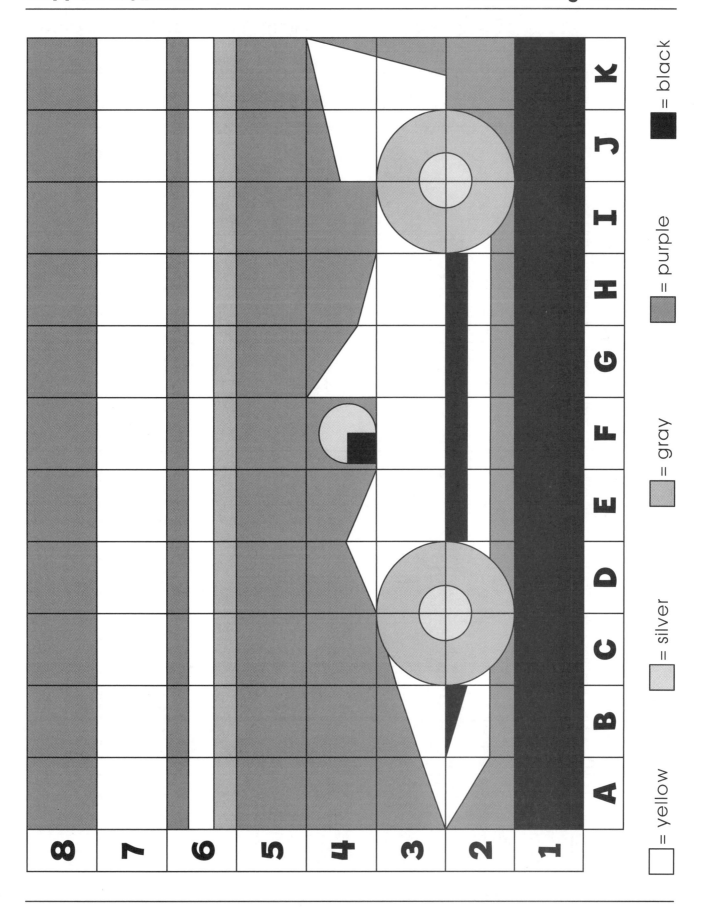

W = white   LB = light blue   LG = light green   DG = dark green
DB = dark blue   Bk = black

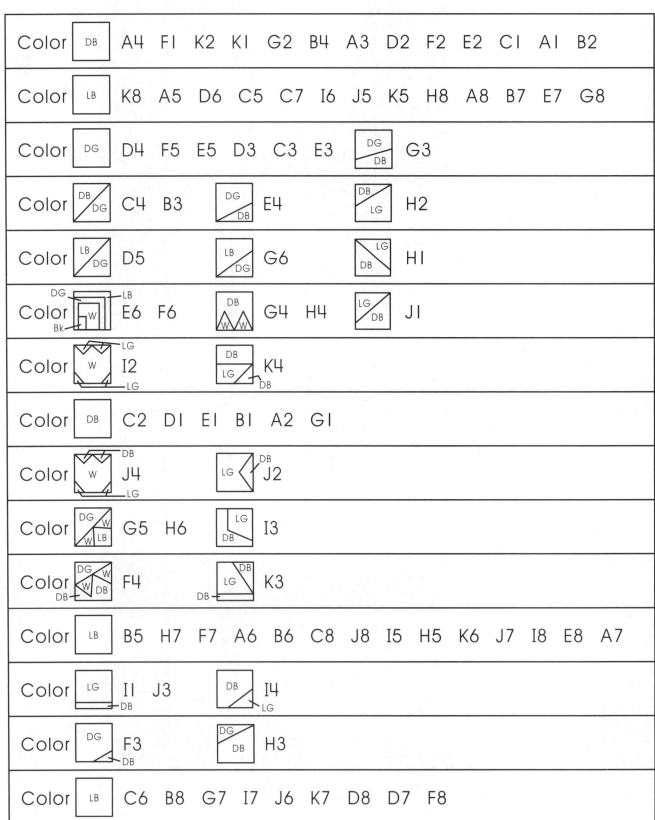

Color [DB] A4 F1 K2 K1 G2 B4 A3 D2 F2 E2 C1 A1 B2

Color [LB] K8 A5 D6 C5 C7 I6 J5 K5 H8 A8 B7 E7 G8

Color [DG] D4 F5 E5 D3 C3 E3 [DG/DB] G3

Color [DB/DG] C4 B3 [DG/DB] E4 [DB/LG] H2

Color [LB/DG] D5 [LB/DG] G6 [LG/DB] H1

Color [DG/LB/W/Bk] E6 F6 [DB/W W] G4 H4 [LG/DB] J1

Color [W/LG] I2 [DB/LG/DB] K4

Color [DB] C2 D1 E1 B1 G1

Color [W/DB/LG] J4 [LG/DB] J2

Color [DG/W/W/LB] G5 H6 [LG/DB] I3

Color [DG/W/DB/DB] F4 [DB/LG/DB] K3

Color [LB] B5 H7 F7 A6 B6 C8 J8 I5 H5 K6 J7 I8 E8 A7

Color [LG/DB] I1 J3 [DB/LG] I4

Color [DG/DB] F3 [DG/DB] H3

Color [LB] C6 B8 G7 I7 J6 K7 D8 D7 F8

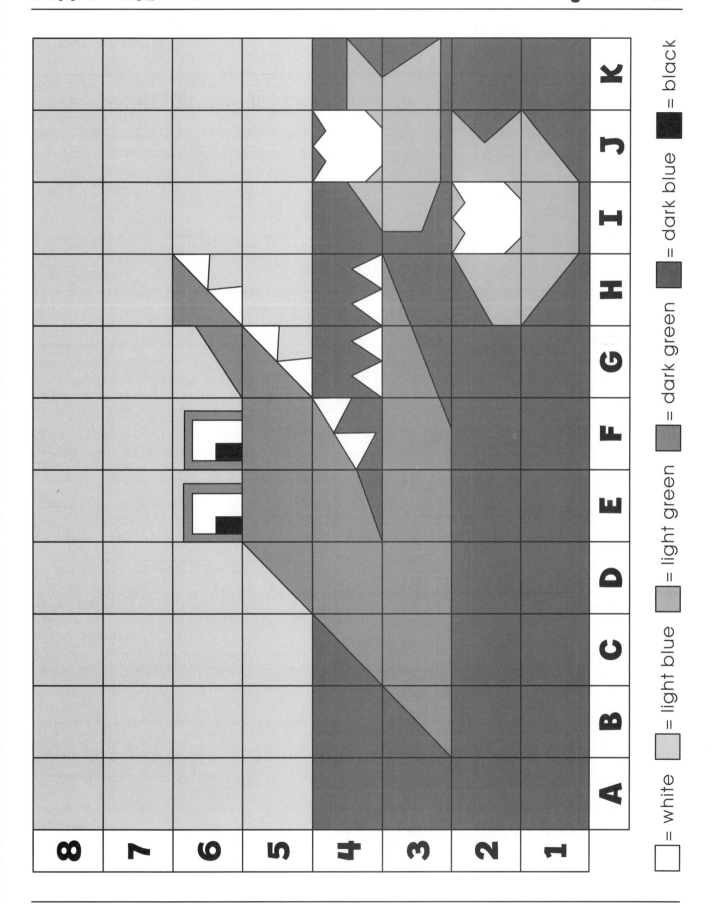

Hidden Picture 13

W = white   B = blue   O = orange   R = red

Bk = black

Color														
Color [B]	K3	F5	A8	B6	A4	F2	F3	A3	B8	E6	E8	F4	A5	A6
Color [W]	B5	C1	B1	E3	E1	A1	I4	J5	J1	K1	H4	G3	D4	C4

Color						
Color [W/Bk Bk] C5		[Bk/W/Bk] C7		[B/R] I8	
Color [B|R] G6		[Bk/W/Bk] D7		[R|B] J7	
Color [B/W] A2		[B/R] H8		[B/W] K2	
Color [W/B] B2	G2	[Bk/R] C8	D8	[R/W/Bk] H7	
Color [W/B] J2	E2	[W/Bk/Bk] H5		[Bk R O] H6	

Color [B]	A7	F6	J8	K8	K7	F7	K5	K4	K6	F8	G8

Color					
Color [W/B] J4	E4	[Bk/Bk R/W] I5		[O W Bk R] I6	
Color [Bk/W/Bk] D5		[O W B] D6		[W/R/Bk] I7	

Color [W]	D2	G5	C3	B3

Color				
Color [B/Bk] B7		[B|R] G7	
Color [Bk/B] E7		[R|B] J6	
Color [B/W] B4	G4	[Bk W O B] C6	

Color [W]	E5	D3	D1	C2	H2	H1	I1	J3	H3	I3	F1	G1	I2

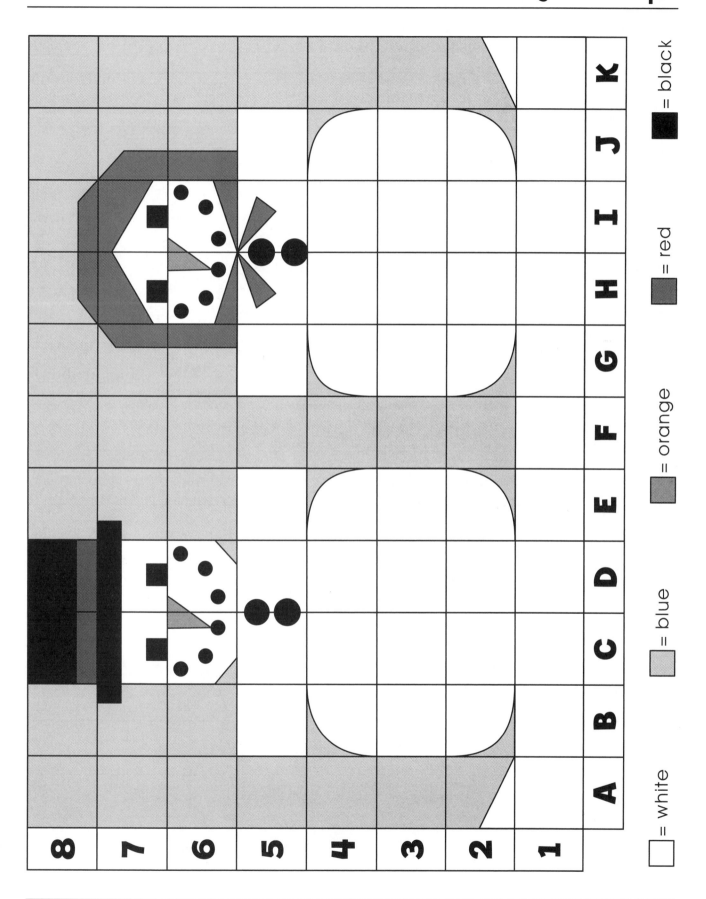

W = white   Y = yellow   O = orange   LG = light green

DG = dark green   Bk = black

Color [O]	B7 D2 C8 F7 E2 E6 D1 D8 C2 E7 E3	
Color [LG]	G2 I8 H7 K1 J8 I1 J7 H2 G7 K7 K8 K5	
Color [Bk]	I3 I6 H4 H5 [DG/O/LG] A2 [LG/Bk] G5	
Color [O/Y] B6 [DG│LG] A8 A1 [O/Bk] F5 [Bk/LG] J6		
Color [DG/LG/O] A7 [Y/O] C3 [Bk/LG] J3		
Color [O/Y] C5 [O/LG] F1 [Bk/Y] D6 D3		
Color [LG/Bk] K3 [LG/Bk] H6 [Y/O] C4		
Color [O] C7 B2 E4 E8 C1 D7 F2 E1 E5		
Color [Bk/LG] K6 [Bk/LG] G3 G6 [Bk/LG] G4		
Color [Y│O] B4 B5 [O/LG] B1 [Bk│LG] J5 J4		
Color [O/Bk] F4 [O/Y] D5 [LG/Bk] H3		
Color [DG│O] A3 A4 A5 A6 [LG/O] B8		
Color [Y/O] D4 [W/Bk/DG] I5 I4 [O/Bk] F3 F6		
Color [LG/O] F8 [Y/O] B3 [O/Y] C6		
Color [LG] G8 I7 J2 H1 I2 J1 G1 K2 H8 K4		

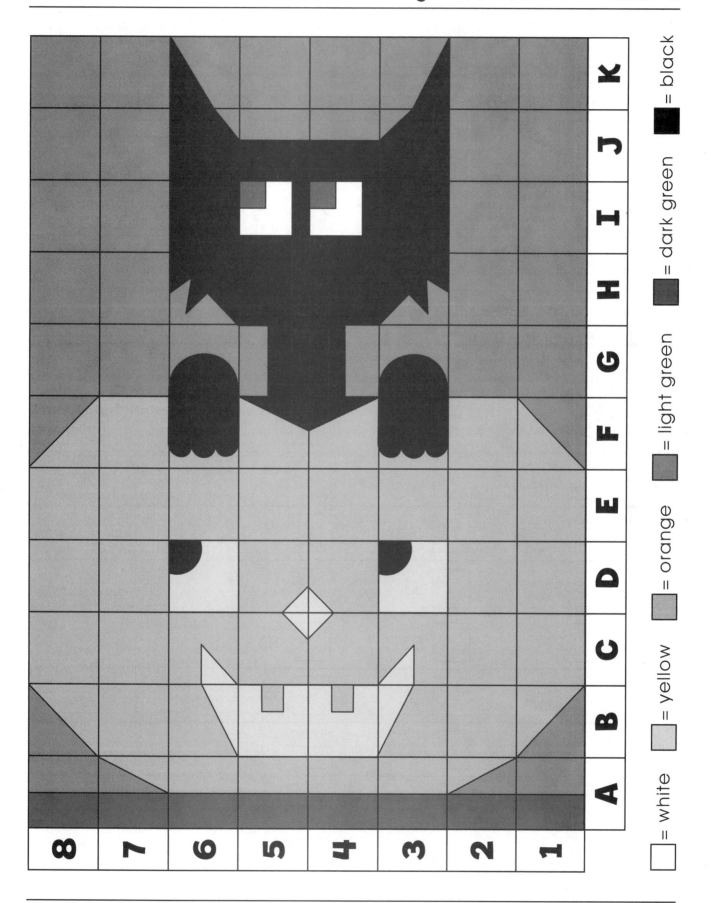

O = orange   Y = yellow   R = red   B = blue
Gn = green   Br = brown   Bk = black

Color [B] K1 C3 K8 D1 C1 C2 D8 K7 K3 F1 G1 I1 E1 J1

Color [Gn] B7 A1 B3 B5 A3 A2 B8 A5 B2 A7 B1 A8

Color [Br] E3 D4 F6 F5 G6 E7 F7 D5 E6 G4 F3

Color [O] H6 I3 I7 H4 J2 J8 G3 I5

Color [R] H2 H8 D3 J7

Color C4 C6 D7 G2

Color A6 A4 H7 H3

Color [B] D2 H1 C7 C8 C5 K2

Color B4 B6 I8 I6

Color E8 J3 I4

Color E2 [Y] K5 K6

Color F2 I2 K4

Color F8 G7 J4

Color H5 G8 J6

Color [Br] D6 E4 E5 F4 G5 J5

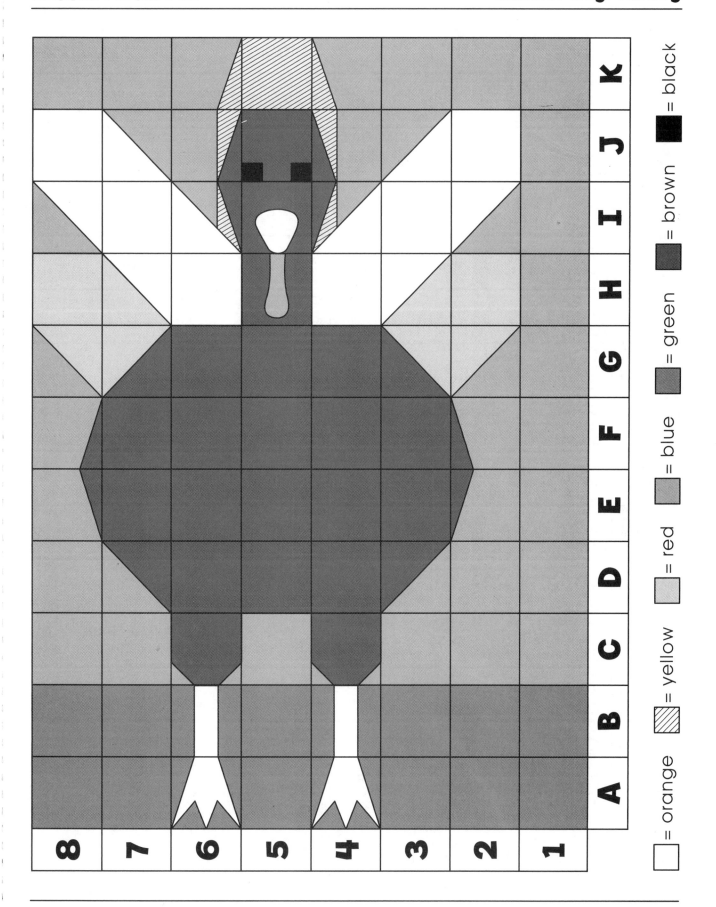

W = white   LB = light blue   R = red   Y = yellow

DB = dark blue   T = tan   Bk = black

Color **[LB]**	A8	C6	K8	J8	E8	D8	C7	B6	B7	A6	A7	C8	B8

Color **[DB]** A4 K4 J4 B4 D4 I4 H4 F4 E4 C4

Color **[T]** AI BI KI JI CI FI HI DI EI GI II

Color **[DB/W]** A3 E3 I3 K3   **[W→T/Y]** G2   **[Y/R]** G7

Color **[DB/W]** F3 H3 J3   **[LB/R]** D6   **[R/Y]** H7

Color **[T]** D2 B2 C3   **[R/LB]** K6

Color **[W/T]** A2 E2 I2 K2   **[R/Y/LB]** E6

Color **[T/W]** F2 H2 J2   **[Y/LB]** F6

Color **[LB/DB]** A5 C5 E5 I5 K5   **[Y/LB]** I6

Color **[LB/DB]** B5 D5 F5 H5 J5   **[DB/Y/W]** G3

Color **[LB/R]** K7 I8   **[DB/Y]** G4   **[T/Bk]** C2

Color **[LB/R]** F8 D7   **[LB/Y/DB]** G5   **[R/Y/LB]** H6

Color **[LB/R]** E7   **[R/Y]** F7   **[Y/R/LB]** J6

Color **[LB/R]** J7   **[R/Y]** I7   **[LB/R/Y/R]** G8

Color **[DB/T/Bk]** D3 B3   **[LB/R/R/Y]** H8   **[Y/R/Y/LB]** G6

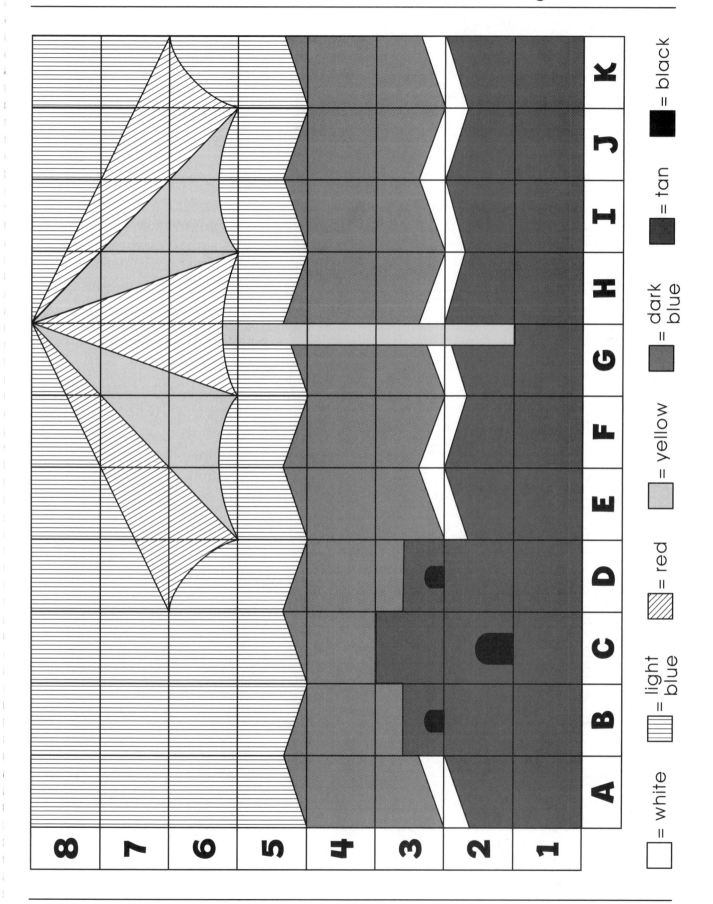

W = white   Y = yellow   Gy = gray   B = blue

Color [B]	A1 J7 K6 I1 J3 A2 A7 J8 G1 D8 C1 E1 G8	
Color [W]	C7 G2 C5 G7 E7 E2 C3 C6 D7 F7 C2 D2 C4	
Color [Gy]	B4 H3 H6 B5 H5 H4 [B/Gy] A5	
Color [B/Gy] H7	[Gy/B] H2	[W Gy B] K5
Color [B Gy] I7	[B/Gy] I6	[B/Gy] B7
Color [Gy B] I2	[Gy/B] I3	[Gy/B] B2
Color [W/Y] D6	[Y/W] F3	[Gy B] B3
Color [B]	K7 I8 A8 K1 J2 J6 J1 K2 K3 K8 F1 D1 B1 B8	
Color [B Gy] A6	[Y] F4 F5	[B Gy] A3
Color [W Y] E6	[Y/W] D3 E3	[Gy B] A4
Color [B Gy] B6	[Gy W] I5	
Color [B]	C8 H8 H1 F8 E8	
Color [Y W] G6	[Gy W] I4	
Color [W/Y] F6	[W Gy B] K4	
Color [W]	J4 G3 J5 G4 G5 F2 D5 E5 D4 E4	

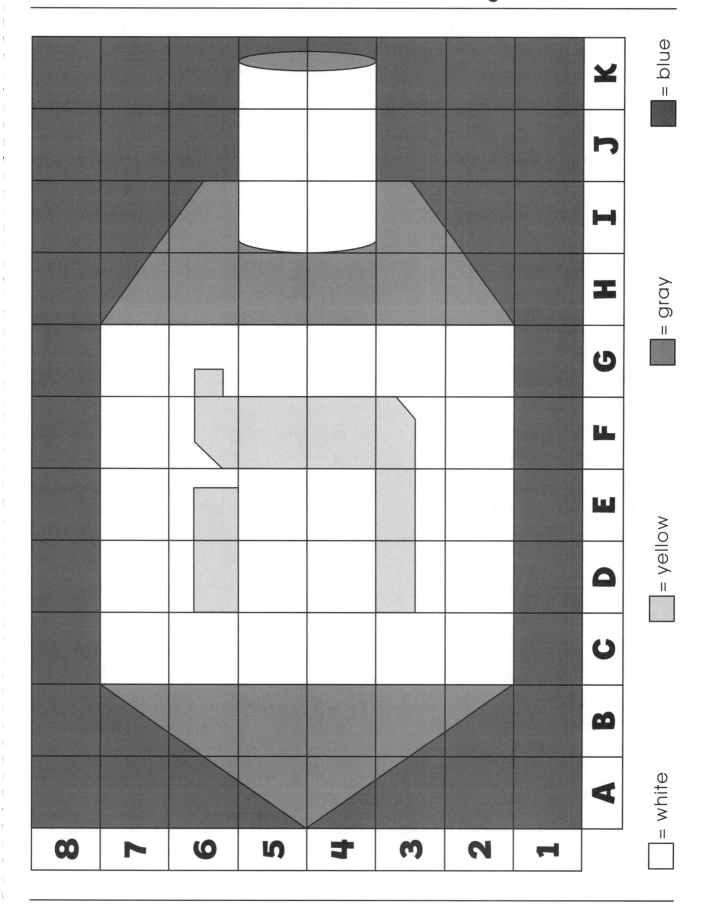

Y = yellow   S = silver   B = blue   Gy = gray
R = red   Bk = black

Color [R]	I4 G3 C4 D5 J4 D4 G4 B4 H4 D6	
Color [Gy]	I1 C1 J1 F1 E1 B1 G1 K1 D1 H1 A1	
Color [B]	J8 G2 J2 A7 E8 H7 K8 I7 C8 E2 G8 B2 F6 E7	
Color [B/Y/B/B] B7	[R/S] B3 J3	[R/B/S] K3
Color [B/Gy] A6	[R/Gy] C6	
Color [Gy/R] B5	[S/R] E3 E4 F3	
Color [S/Bk/B] I2 D2	[R/B] K4	[S/Bk/B] C2 H2
Color [B] K2 J7 B8 H8 E6 F7 A2 K7 A8 I8 F5		
Color [Gy/R] C5	[B/R/S] A3	[R/S] F4
Color [R/B/Bk] K5		
Color [R/Gy] B6	[Bk/R/S] D3 I3	
Color [B] C7 D8 F2 G7 F8 E5		
Color [B/Gy/R] A5	[B/Bk] G6 H6 I6 J6 K6	
Color [B/Y] D7	[R/Bk] G5 H5 I5 J5	
Color [R/Bk/S] C3 H3	[B/Y/R] A4	

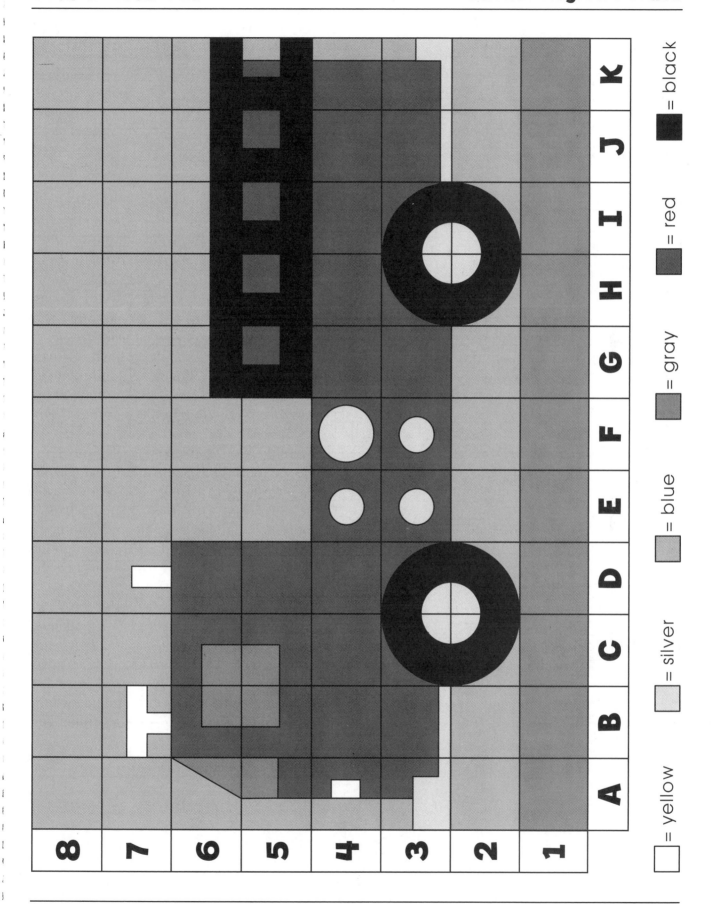

W = white   LG = light green   B = blue   Y = yellow
Pk = pink   DG = dark green   Bk = black

Color [B] A8 D3 I4 A6 J8 K8 A7 B8 A4 E3 I8 K5

Color [DG] K1 J1 I1 H1 E1 F1 A1 B1 C1 D1 G1

Color [Y] E8 E4   [W/B] I3   [B/DG] E2   [LG/W/Y] G5

Color [B/W/LG] C7   [DG/B] C3   [B/W/DG] G2   [W/Pk] C6   [Bk/LG/W/Bk] C5

Color [W/Y/B] H5   [Pk/B/DG] J5   [B/DG] B3   [Y/B] F4   [W/Pk/B] H7

Color [B/DG] I2 K2   [B/Y] F8   [W/B] C2   [Bk/B/W/Bk] H6   [B/Y] D8

Color [LG] E7   [W/B/DG] B4   [B/DG/DG] J4   [W/Y/B] D4   [W/B/DG] H2

Color [B] A5 C8 I5 I7 F3 K7   [B/W/Pk] H8   [B/Y] G4   [Y/Pk] J6

Color [B/DG] J2   [B/DG] A2   [Pk/W/LG] G7   [B/B/Pk] J7

Color [W/B/DG] C4   [Pk/W/B] B6   [B/Pk/B] I6   [Y/W/B] G3   [Pk/W/Bk/Bk] G6

Color [Pk/B/B] K6   [Y/W/B] H3   [B/DG] F2   [Pk] D6 F6 E6

Color [Pk/W/B] B7 G8   [B/B/DG] K4   [B/W/Bk] B5   [DG/B] K3

Color [B/W] A3   [Y/B] H4   [B] D2   [DG/B] J3

Color [B/W] B2   [LG/W] F5   [LG] E5 D7 F7 D5

Draw mouths and whiskers.

 Graphing Hidden Pictures

Graphing Hidden Pictures

W = white   Y = yellow   O = orange   R = red   B = blue

Color [B]	B8 G2 H3 D8 H8 I6 K5 J5 A1 F8 G3 I3 G8 I5	
Color [Y]	C3 C4 C5	A6
Color [W]	J4 G4 H4 I4	
Color [R]	B6 F4 B2	D4
Color [B]	F7 H6 C8 G6 H5 K2 J2 E8 G5 I7 J8 H1 J7 H7	
Color [O]	E6 E2	F5 E5
Color	D1 E1	B1 C1 F3
Color	B7	E4 D2
Color	A5	A3 A4 C7 D7 E7
Color	B4 B3 C6 D6	D5
Color [B]	G1 A7 G7 I2 K3 J3 F1 A8 H2 I8 I1 K1 J6 J1	
Color	F2	K4
Color	A2	D3 B5
Color	C2	F6 E3
Color [B]	K6 K7 K8	

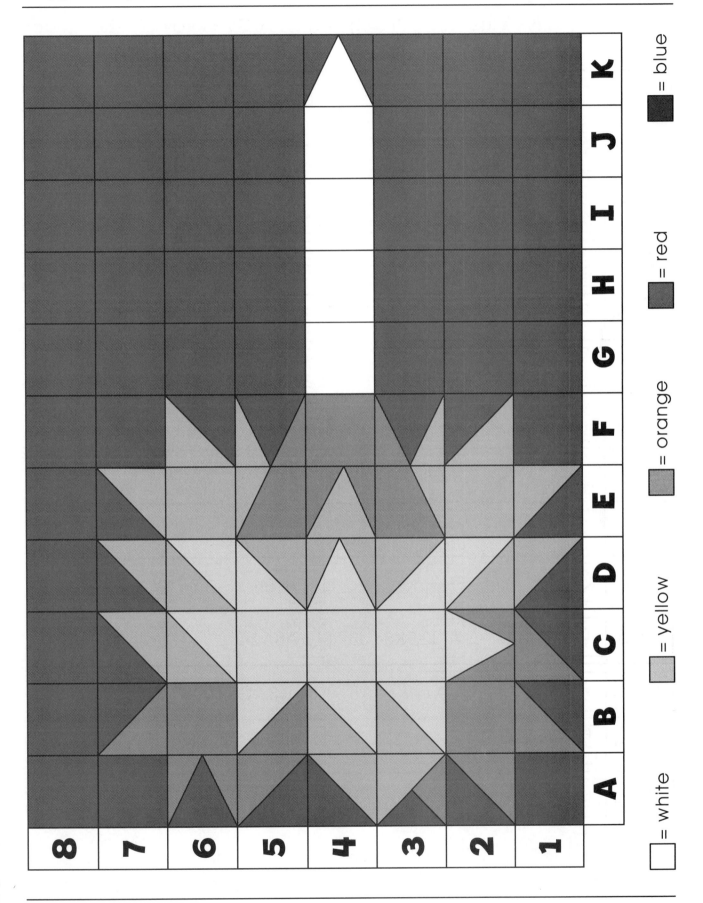

= blue

= red

= orange

= yellow

= white

W = white   B = blue   Gn = green   Gy = gray   Bk = black

Color	[Gn]	J2 H1 K2 I1 B1 K1 I2 D1 J1 E1 F1
Color	[Gy]	F3 G5 E4 H5 F5 E3 [B/Bk] J8 [Gy/Gn] B2 D2
Color	[B/Gy/Bk] I7	[Gy/B/Gn] I3 [Gy/B/W] D6 [Gy/Gn] C2
Color	[B/Gy/W] A6	[B/Gy] C6 [W/B/Gy] A3 [Gy/W] B5
Color	[Gy/B/Bk] J7	[W/Gy] D3 [Gy/Gn] F2 [Bk/Gy/B] J4
Color	[Gy/Bk] I6 J6 I5	[Gy/W/Bk/Gy] C4 [B/Gy] B6 [Gy/B] A5
Color	[W/Bk/Gy] D4	[B/Gy] F6 [Gy/Gn] E2 [B/Bk] I8
Color	[B]	C7 B8 E7 E8 K4 B7 D7 H7 H8 K5
Color	[B/Gy] H6	[Gy/W] C5
Color	[Gy/Bk] I4	[B/Gn] K3 J3 [W/Bk/Gy/Gy] B4
Color	[Gy/Gn] H2	[W/Gy/Bk] B3 [Gn/Gy] A2
Color	[B]	C8 F7 F8 A7 K6 K8 A8 D8 G7 G8 K7
Color	[Bk/Gn] A1 C1 G1	[B/Gy] E6
Color	[W/Bk/Gy] C3	[Gy/Bk] J5 [B/W/Bk] A4
Color	[Gy]	G3 H4 G6 G2 E5 F4 G4 H3 D5

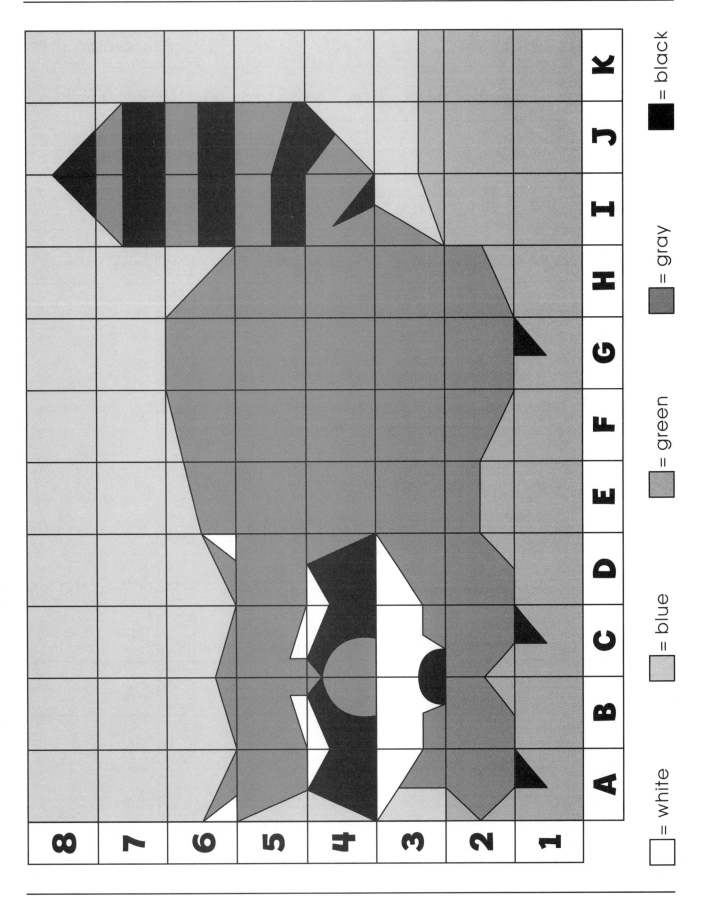

■ = black

■ = gray

■ = green

■ = blue

□ = white

Y = yellow   DB = dark blue   O = orange   LB = light blue
Gn = green   R = red   Br = brown   Bk = black

Color [LB]   A1   E8   K1   B2   G7   I6   C1   F2   F8   G1   H1   H7   K5   B1

Color [Gn]   G5   F5   F6   E6   [Gn/R] H5   [R/LB/DB] J4

Color [Y]   G3   [Gn/O/R] E5   [O/LB] I1   [R/Y] I4

Color [DB]   J3   [LB/Br] F1   [O/LB/Br] E2   [LB/DB/R] C5

Color [DB/LB/Bk/Y] K3   [Y/LB] H3   [LB/Gn] H6   [Gn/R/Y] H4

Color [DB/DB/O] J2   [LB/Gn] F7   [R/O/LB] C4   [O/LB/Br/LB] C3

Color [Y/Gn] F4   [LB/R] D3   [Br/LB] B5   [Br/LB] A4

Color [LB]   J5   H8   D8   J6   K7   A6   A3   D1   H2   C8   A7   G8   I7   A2

Color [LB/R] I5   [Br/LB] E1   [Br/O/LB] D2   [LB/LB/DB] A8   [O/LB] J1

Color [Br/O/LB] B3   [DB/LB] K2   [Y/DB/LB] I3   [LB/DB] B6   [Br/LB] C2

Color [DB/LB] B7   [LB/DB] B8   [LB/Br] A5   [R/Y/LB] D4

Color [LB/Gn] E7   [LB/DB/Gn] C7   [Y/R/LB] E3   [DB/LB] C6

Color [Gn/DB] D6   [LB/DB] K4   [Gn/Y] G4   [Br/O/LB] B4

Color [DB/LB] I2   [LB/Gn] G6   [Y/LB] F3   [O/R] D5

Color [LB]   G2   I8   J7   J8   K6   K8   [LB/Gn/Gn] D7   [R/Y] E4

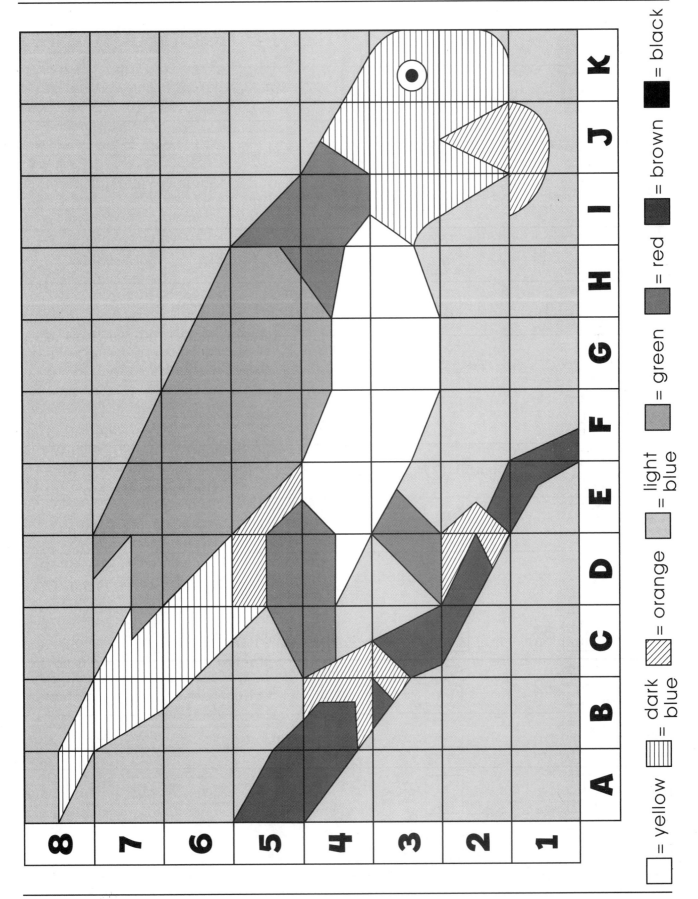

Gn = green   LB = light blue   Gy = gray   DB = dark blue
Bk = black

Color [LB] F8 G8 A8 B8 K8 H8 C8 I8 J8

Color [DB] F5 F6 J5 J6 C5 C6 A6 C1 D1 E1 G5 G6

Color [Bk] C3 D5 D4 E4 E3 D3 G4 C4 E5 H3

Color [Bk/DB] H4   [DB/Gn/DB] G1 B1 A2 B5 K1 K3 I1 K5

Color [Gn/DB/Bk] B4   [DB/Bk] E6   [Gn/DB/DB] F1 J1

Color [DB/DB/Gn] I2 K6 A5 B6   [Gn/DB/DB] B2 A1 K4 K2

Color [Gy/LB/DB/Bk] E7   [DB/Bk] J4   [Bk/DB] D2 E2

Color [LB/DB] K7 I7 A7 C7 G7   [Bk/DB] I3

Color [Bk/DB] C2   [DB/Bk] I4   [DB/DB/Gn] H1

Color [Bk/DB] J3   [LB/Gy] E8   [DB/DB/Gn/Bk] A4

Color [DB/Bk] D6   [Gn/Bk/DB/DB] A3   [DB] H5 H6 I5 I6

Color [Bk/DB] H2   [Bk/Bk/DB/DB/Gn] G2   [DB/DB/Gn] J2

Color [LB/Gy] D8   [LB/DB] F7 J7 H7 B7 D7

Color [Bk/Gn/Bk/DB/DB] F2   [Bk/Gn/DB] B3

Color [Gn/Bk/Bk] F3   [Bk/Bk/Gn] G3 F4

Answer Key: Submarine

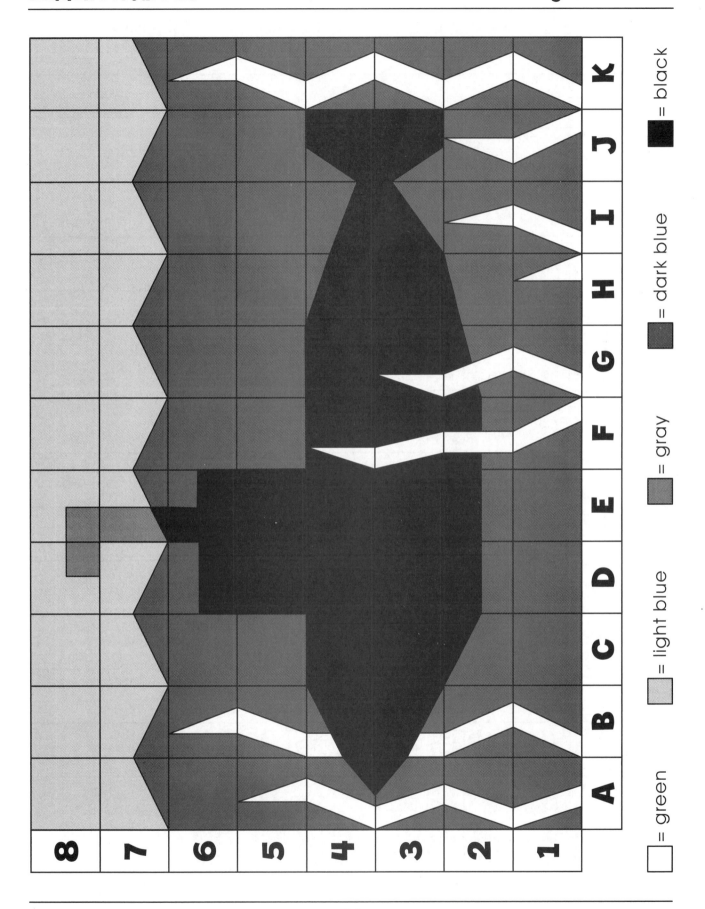

Y = yellow   Pk = pink   Gn = green   B = blue
Pl = purple

| Color | B | A8 | I2 | D2 | J7 | K8 | K7 | K2 | C2 | C7 | B8 | I8 | I7 | D8 | DI |

| Color | Pk | D4 | C5 | C6 | B3 | A4 | A5 | B4 | D5 | C4 | B5 | C3 | B6 |

Color E8   F7 F3 I5 EI

Color A6   D6   H3

Color E4   D3   H5

Color F8 I6 A3   H2 K4

Color G8 J6   E7   H7 K5

| Color | B | CI | B2 | A7 | D7 | J8 | KI | II | BI | AI | A2 | B7 | JI | J2 | C8 |

Color G4   E3   H8 K6

Color G7 J5 G3   K3 HI

Color G6 J4 G2   F4

Color G5 GI J3   H6

Color F5   E6   H4

Color I3 FI   E5

Color F6 F2 I4   E2

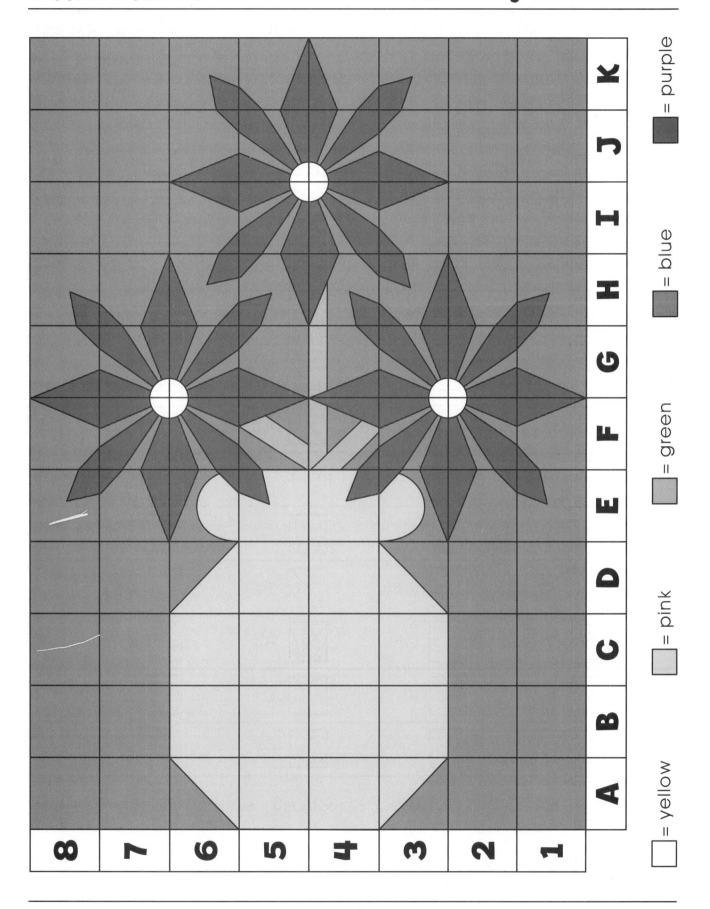

= purple

= blue

= green

= pink

= yellow

B = blue   LG = light green   T = tan   DG = dark green

Br = brown   Bk = black

| Color | B | A2 E7 K1 K8 D7 B8 J1 I2 H3 F7 C8 K7 B7 F2 |

Color [B] I5   [LG/B] I4   [T/Br] E5   [B/Br] C2

Color [DG] H7 G8 J5   [B/Br/B] D1   [B/T] B6

Color [T] D3 C3   [T/B] B4   [Br/T] A5   [B/T] A4

Color [Br] F5   [DG/B] G7   [B/DG] H8 I8   [B/T] D4

Color [DG/B/LG] J8   [Br/LG] I6   [Br/B/Bk/Br/T] G4   [B/B/T/Bk] F4

Color [LG/B] J7 J3   [B/T] E6 D6   [B/T] A6   [B/T] E4

| Color | B | B1 C7 E8 K3 A1 A8 K5 F6 G1 I1 H1 H2 J2 K4 |

Color [T/B] E3   [B/Br] H6   [Bk/Br/Br/B/T] G3   [B/T] C6

Color [B/Br/B] B2   [B/Br] G6   [DG/LG] J4   [Br/T] B5

Color [DG/Br] I7   [Br/B] G5   [B/T/Br/B] B3   [Br/T] C5

Color [B/Br/DG] J6   [Br/B] H5   [Br/B/B] C1   [T/B/T] C4

Color [B/DG] F8   [Br/T] D5   [T/Bk/B/B] F3

Color [B/LG] H4 I3   [B] A7 D8 G2 A3 K2 K6 D2 E1 E2 F1

Turn the paper. Draw eyes and a mouth.

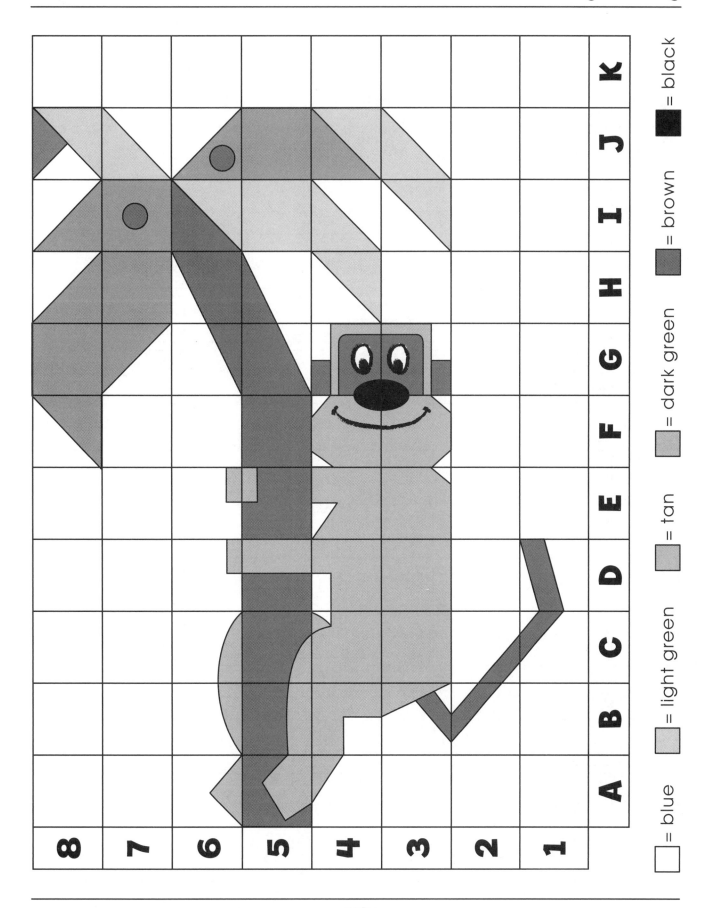

W = white   Y = yellow   LB = light blue   DB = dark blue
R = red   BG = blue-green   Bk = black

Color [LB]	E1	I7	J6	K1	G1	F8	D8	H6	I8	K5	K6	J8	H7	G7
Color [DB]	A8	B7	A6	B5	A4	A7	B8	B6	A5	B4				
Color [BG]	A2	B1	C3	D3	D4	B2	A1	C2	[◻] G3					

Color [R/LB] J3	[Y/R/LB] I3	[LB/W/BG] D6	[R/Bk] F3
Color [Y] H4	[LB/W] E7	[LB/DB/BG] C4	[Y/LB/R] F5
Color [LB/DB] C8 C6	[Y/R] F4	[BG/DB] A3	[R/Bk/LB] F2
Color [LB/R] G5	[Y/Bk] H3	[BG/Y/LB] D2	[R/Y] H5

Color [LB]	E8	G6	F1	H1	I2	J1	J7	K8	H8	G8	I6	I1	K7	F7

Color [W/BG/Y/LB] E6	[LB/R] K3	[BG/Y] E4	[Y/LB/R] J5
Color [BG/Y/LB] C1	[Y/R/Bk/LB] E2	[BG/Y] E5	[R/LB] J4
Color [DB/BG] B3	[LB] K4	[LB/Y] I5	[LB/R] J2
Color [DB/LB] C7	[LB/W] D7	[Y/R] I4	
Color [DB/LB/W] C5	[Bk/LB] H2	[Y/LB] D1	
Color [W/BG] D5	[LB/Y] F6	[Bk/LB] G2	
Color [R/Bk/Y] G4	[BG/Y/Bk] E3	[R/LB/LB] K2	

W = white   S = silver   Y = yellow   Gn = green
R = red   Gy = gray   Bk = black

Color [Gy]	DI	AI	JI	II	FI	GI	EI	HI	KI	BI	CI			
Color [Gn]	C8	K6	E2	A6	F2	J8	B6	K7	A4	H2	E8	F8	D7	
Color [Y]	E6	[Bk/Gn] B2	I2	[W/Bk/W] I5	[Gn/Y] F7									
Color [W]	G3	H4	J4	[Bk/Gn] K2	D2	[Gn/R] A5								
Color [Bk]	J2	C2	K3	I3	[Bk/S/Y] G7	[W/Bk/R] C5								
Color [S/Bk/Gn] H7	[Bk/Y/W/R] D5	[W/Bk] I4	[Y/Bk/W] F3										
Color [Gn/W] K5	[Gy/Gn] A3	[Gn/Y/R/Y] G6	[W/Gn/Bk] K4										
Color [Gn]	B8	K8	G2	A7	J7	D8	A2	I8	J6	B7	C6	C7	A8	
Color [Gn] J5	[W/R/Y] E4	[Y/W/R] F4	[Gn/Y] D6										
Color [W/Gn/Bk] I6	[Bk/R/W] D4	[Gn/Bk] G8	[Y/W/R] G5										
Color [Gy/Bk] B3	[W/Gn] H3	[Y/R/W] H5	[Gn/Bk/R/Y/R] H6										
Color [W/R] G4	[Bk/W/R/Bk] C4	[Gn/Y] E7	[Gn/W/R] B5										
Color [Gn/Bk] H8	[Y/R] F6	[Bk/W/Gy/Bk] D3	[R/Y/Y/W] F5										
Color [Gy/S/Bk/Bk] C3	[Y/W] E5	[Gn/W] I7											
Color [W/Bk/Gn/Bk] B4	[Bk/Y/Bk/W] E3	[Bk/W/Bk/S/Bk/Bk] J3											

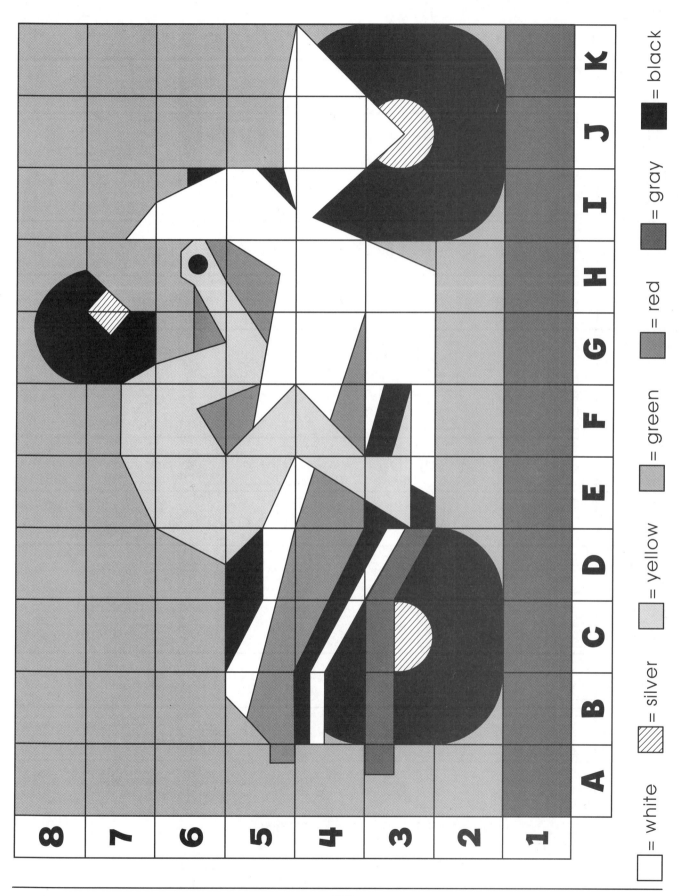

W = white   Br = brown   R = red   Y = yellow
LG = light green   O = orange   DG = dark green   Bk = black

Color [Y]	J7 J8 E6	I4	[W] J2 K2	
Color [O]	I3 I2	J3	F3	
Color [DG]	B5 B6 K6 K5 K4	E4		
Color [LG]	H6 H5 GI HI BI CI EI DI AI FI II			
Color [Br]	E2 F8 G8 C8 D8 A8 I8			
Color [LG]	H7	D2	B4	
Color	K3	H8 E8 B8		
Color	I7 I5 C3 C5 D6	F2		
Color [Y]	E5	D5	K7 J6 J5 K8	
Color	F7 B3 F5 A6 A2 C6 G6 A3 A5 A7 G3			
Color	JI KI	B7	A4	
Color	F4	H4	D3	
Color	E7	D4	G5 B2 G7 F6	
Color	G4	G2 H3 C2 I6 D7 C4 C7		
Color	H2	J4	E3	

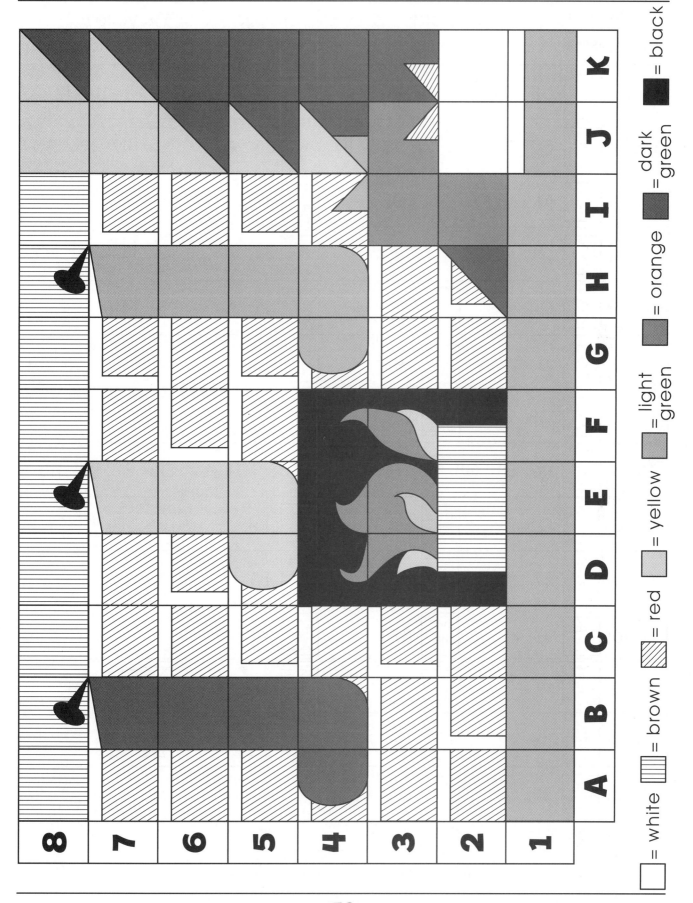

LB = light blue   Go = gold   O = orange   Y = yellow
Gn = green   R = red   DB = dark blue   Bk = black

Color	LB	D8 K5 H7 J7 I8 HI E3 F8 D2 EI G2 F3 II H2

Color	Bk	C7 B6 A5 C5 C6 B7 A6 B5 A7 LB I7 J6 G3

Color	Gn	BI A3 A2 B3 B2 AI H3

Color	Gn / LB	CI C2 C3 E6 G4

Color	C4	H5 I3 H6

Color	JI	F4 K2 I5

Color	C8	D7 J4 J5

Color	LB	K6 E8 G8 DI F2 D4 K7 J8 GI E2 D3 FI K8 H8

Color	G5	D6 K4 I4

Color	E7	A8 F5 KI

Color	D5	A4 F6 I6

Color	F7	J2 G7 J3

Color	B8	I2 G6 K3

Color	B4	H4

Color	E5	E4

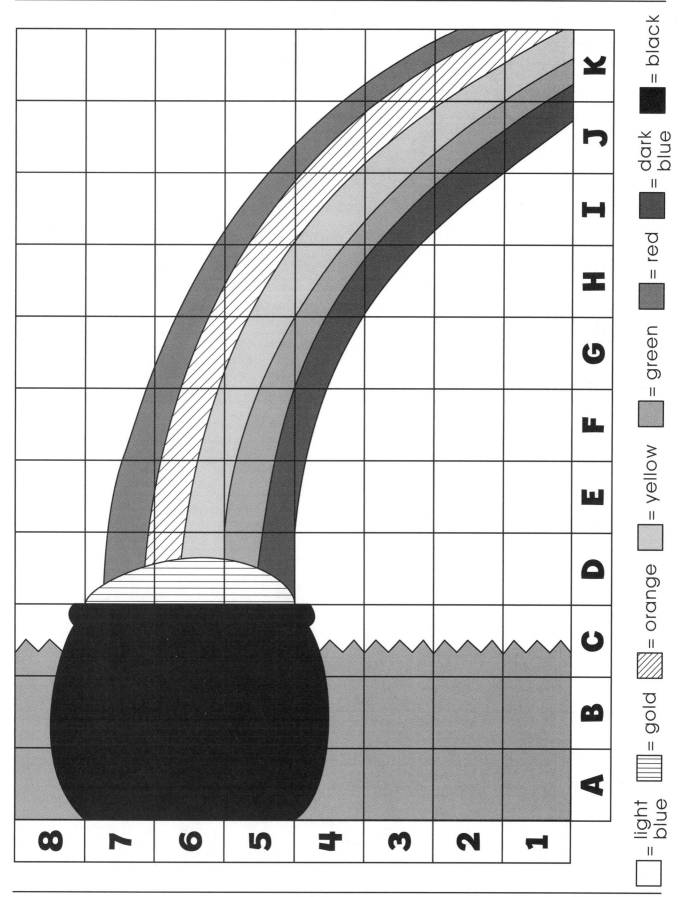

Hidden Picture 30

Directions

B = blue   Y = yellow   O = orange   Gn = green
Pl = purple   Bk = black

Color	B	B3	E8	A1	H7	K5	J8	D8	B2	F8	H8	A3	I1	K6

Color	O	G4	G3	E2	E3	C5	D4

Color	Pl	J5	J3	F5	E6	F7

Color	B5	G5	D5	C1

Color	J2	J6	A6

Color	D3	I5	H5

Color	F3	A5	J4	E1

Color	B	A2	E7	G7	G8	K3	K4	C2	H1	A8	I7	K1	K2	J7	B7

Color	E5	D2	G6	B6

Color	C6	I2	H4	D6

Color	F1	I6

Color	H2	D1	F2	F6	F4

Color	H6	H3	I4	C7

Color	G1	C4	E4	I3	G2

Color	B	I8	B1	K7	K8	J1	B8	A7	A4	D7	C3	C8	B4

© Carson-Dellosa • CD-104283   **62**   Graphing Hidden Pictures

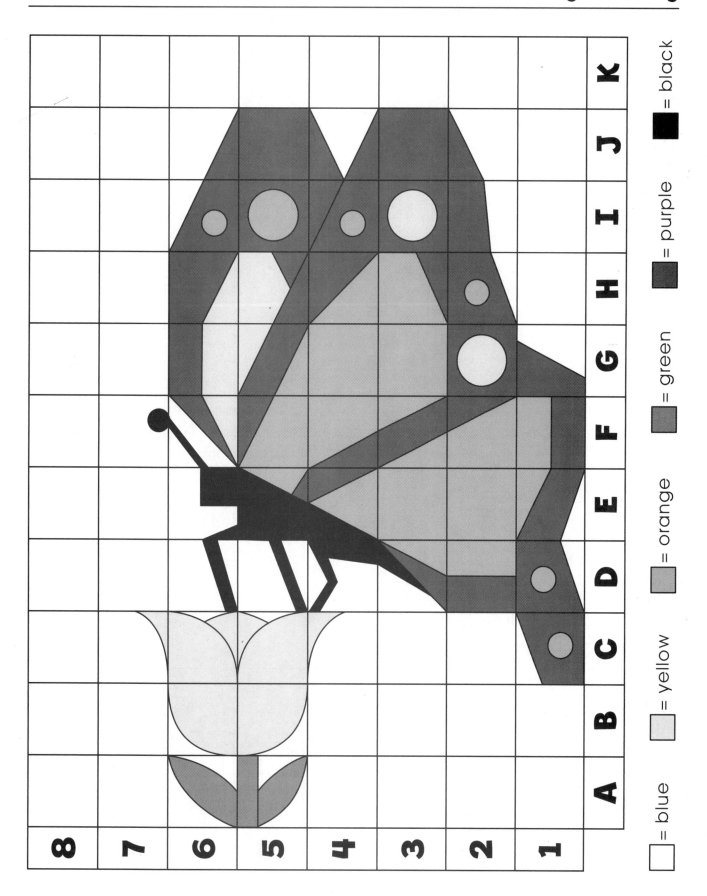

Name: _____

Hidden Picture: _____

	A	B	C	D	E	F	G	H	I	J	K
8											
7											
6											
5											
4											
3											
2											
1											

© Carson-Dellosa • CD-104283